T.D. MACDONALD (1864-1937)
was a writer and poet with a deep interest
in Scots and Gaelic language. As well as
gathering proverbs for this collection,
Thomas Donald MacDonald wrote
The Lords of Lochaber,
Celtic Dialects, Dain Eadar-
Theangaichte, Dain an am Chogaidh
and *Dain an Deidh a Chogaidh.*

Do not pluck
the beard of a stranger

...and other wise Gaelic proverbs

Collected by

T.D. MACDONALD

Selected by

LUATH PRESS

Luath Press Limited

EDINBURGH

www.luath.co.uk

First published 2018

ISBN: 978-1-910745-40-3

Proverbs sourced from:
Gaelic Proverbs and Proverbial Sayings
by T.D. MacDonald published
by Eneas Mackay, Stirling 1926

The paper used in this book is recyclable. It is made
from low chlorine pulps produced in a low energy,
low emission manner from renewable forests.

Printed and bound by T.J. International, Padstow

Design by Tom Bee

Typeset in Mayflower by 3btype.com

CONTENTS

MONEY
AND
WORK

Uaisle gun chuid,
is maragain gun gheir.

Birth without means,
and puddings without suet.

*Those born without money
are at a disadvantage.*

An ràmh is fhaisg air
laimh, iomair leis.

The oar that's nearest,
row with it.

Use what you have.

An ràthad fada glan,
is an ràthad
goirid salach.

The long clean road,
and the short dirty road.

*If you want something to happen
quickly you might have to cut corners.*

Bidh an ùbhal is fhearr air a mheangan is àirde.

The best apple will be
on the highest bough.

*What is the worthiest to achieve
requires the most effort.*

Cha'n fheum an ti
a shealbhaicheas
an toradh am blàth
a milleadh.

He who would enjoy the fruit
must not spoil the blossom.

*You have to work hard to get
the best outcome.*

Cha'n uaisle duine na cheird.

No man is above his trade.

Nobody is too good to work.

Cha deanar buanachd gun chall.

There is no profit without loss.

There is no reward without sacrifice.

Am fear nach cui ri là fuar, Cha bhuan e ri là teth.

He who will not sow
on a cold day will not reap
on a warm day.

You have to put in the work
regardless of the circumstances
to reach your goal.

Am fear a theid a gnà a mach le lion Gheibh e eun uaireigin.

He who always sets his net
will get a bird sometime.

*If you are persistent, patient
and prepared you will be rewarded.*

Cha do shoirbhich
dithis riamh aìr an
aon chnoc.

Two never prospered
on the same hill.

Space is needed to prosper.

Is fhearr caitheamh
na meirgeadh.

Better wear than rust.

Work hard or else decay.

Bheir an èigin air rud-eigin a dheanamh.

Necessity is the mother
of invention.

*When you are in need
you will find a solution.*

Cluinnidh am bodhar fuaim an airgead.

The deaf will hear
the clink of money.

Everyone values money.

Eallach mhòr an duine leisg.

The heavy burden
of the lazy man.

*The lazy will claim
everything is difficult.*

Am foar nach dean
baile air a bheagan,
Cha'n aìridh e air
a mhòran.

He who does not work
the small farm is unworthy
of a big one.

*You have to start from the bottom
and work your way up.*

Cha bhi toradh
gun saothar.

There will be no
produce without labour.

Work to see results.

Cha leasachadh air
droch obair-làtha
A bhi fada gum
toiseachadh.

A late beginning will not mend
a bad day's work.

*Sleeping in
will not fix a bad day.*

Is fhearr làn an dùirn de cheird na làn an dùirn a dh'òir.

Better a handful of
craftsmanship
than a handful of gold.

*Money does not make you happy,
work does.*

Is fhearr sior obair na sàr obair.

Better steady work
than severe spurts of work.

Do not procrastinate.

Se cleachdadh
a nì teòmachd.

Experience makes expertness.

Having experience makes you more knowledgeable in your field.

Am fear a bhios fada
gun èiridh,
bidh e na leum fad'
an làtha.

He who is late in rising
will be in a hurry all day.

There's no making up for a late start.

FRIENDSHIP
AND
LOVE

An rud a théid fad
o'n t-sùil théid e fad
o'n chrìdhe.

What goes far from the eye
will go far from the heart.

Distance destroys love.

Cha sheas càirdeas
air a lèth-chois.

Friendship
will not stand on one leg.

*It takes two
to make a friendship function.*

Ceilichidh seirc aineamh.

Friendship
conceals blemishes.

*A friend's flaws
are easy to ignore.*

Am fear a ghleidheas
a theanga
gleidhidh e a charaid.

He who holds his tongue
keeps his friend.

*Know when to stay quiet
if you want to keep your friends.*

Is treise dithis
a dol thar an atha,
na fad'o' chèile.

Two are stronger together,
than far apart
in crossing a ford.

*It is easier to overcome problems
together than alone.*

Is minig a bha pòsadh
luath na pòsadh
truagh, is am posadh
mall na pòsadh dall.

The hurried marriage is often
a tragedy, and the slow to marry
are often blind.

*Be discerning in your choice
of partner, but not so picky
you wait forever.*

Na gabh te air
bith mar mnai
a sheallas i fhèin
gun mheang.

Take no woman
for a wife who presents herself
without a flaw.

No one is perfect.

Na chì na bige
'se ni na bige,
na chluinneas iad
'se chanas iad.

What the little ones will see
the little ones will do,
and what they hear
they will repeat.

Children will copy adults.

Tagh do bhean 's a currachd-oidch' oirre.

Choose your wife
with her night-cap on.

*You should see your spouse
at their worst
before you marry them.*

Cha sgeul rùin e is
fios aig triuir air.

It is no secret
when three know it.

*A secret should be kept
between two people.*

Bu mhath an sgàthan sùil caraid.

A friend's eye
is a good looking-glass.

*Friends see you clearly and speak
about you honestly.*

Furan an t-aoidh a thig, greas an t-aoidh tha fálbh.

Welcome the coming,
speed the parting guest.

*Guests are welcome,
but so is their departure.*

Fàgaidh siod, is sròl,
is sgàrlaid,
gun teinne, gun tuar
an fhàrdach.

Silk and satin, and scarlet,
leave a fireless, colourless hearth.

The material does not make you happy.

Teinne chaoran
is gaol ghiullan,
cha do mhair iad
fada riamh.

Peat-fragment fire
and boy's love
never were lasting.

Puppy love never lasts.

Theid dùthchas an aghaidh na'n creag.

Kinship
will withstand the rocks.

*Family
will outlast hard times.*

An leanabh a dh'
fhàgar dha fhéin.
cuiridh e air a
mhàthair nàire.

The child that's left to himself
will put his mother to shame.

Unwatched children will misbehave.

Comhairle caraid
gun iarraidh,
cha d'fhuair I riamh a
mheas bu choir d'ì.

A friend's counsel,
unasked, is never esteemed
as it ought to be.

*A friend's unprompted opinion
is not appreciated.*

Cha bi an t-suiridh bean gun chosdas.

Wooing is a costly dame.

Love is expensive.

Fàinne mu'n mheur
's gun snàithne
mu'n mhàs.

A ring on the finger
and no clothes on the loins.

*A veneer of respectability
sometimes hides bad character.*

Tagh nighean an
deagh mháthair ged
a b'e an Diabhuil
a h-athair

Choose the good mother's
daughter were the
devil her father.

*Upbringing will affect the child
more than parentage.*

NATURE
AND
WEATHER

Se 'n èigin
a chuir an earb
thar an loch.

Necessity made the roe
swim across the loch.

*When you need something
you go to extremes to get it.*

Eiridh tonn
air uisge balbh.

Waves will rise
on silent water.

*A violent storm may occur
when everything
is at its calmest.*

Feumaidh
na fithichean fhéin
a bhi beò.

Even the ravens
must live.

*Every being
has the right to live.*

Tachraidh na daoine,
ach cha tachair
na cnuic.

Men will meet,
but the hills will not.

Friendship is always possible,
in the scheme of things.

Is math an
seirbheiseach teine,
ach's olc a
mhaighstir e.

Fire is a good servant,
but a bad master.

*Keep careful control of fire,
it is as dangerous as it is useful.*

Aìteamh na gaoth tuath, sneach is reodhadh anns an uair.

The thaw that comes while north winds blow will be followed by frost and snow.

Do not trust something unexpectedly good, there might be difficulties ahead.

Am fear nach cuir
ʿs a mhàirt
cha bhuan e ʿs an
Fhoghair.

Who doesn't sow in March
will not reap in Autumn.

You have to do the work
in order to see results.

An sneach nach tig
mu shamhuinn
thig e gu reamhar mu
Fheill-Brìghde.

The snow that comes not
at Hallowmas, will come thickly
at Candlemas.

*The bad weather
will arrive eventually.*

Breac a mhuiltein air
an àthar –
bidh là math a
màireach ann.

There is a dappled
sky to-day, there will be
a good day to-morrow.

*A cloudy sky one day
means good weather the next.*

Tha'n cat 's an luath, thig frasan fuar.

The cat is in the ashes,
cold showers are coming.

*A Gaelic superstition
that if a cat sits with its back
to the fireplace, snow is coming.*

Tha'n seillein
fo dhion,
Thig gaillionn is sìan.

The bee has taken shelter,
a storm and rain are coming.

*When the bees hide away
the summer is over.*

Fàs a ghrunnd
-air reir an uachdraìn.

The yield of the ground
will depend on the landlord.

The results of your work
are your responsibility.

PERSONALITIES

A bhò is miosa
'th' anns a bhuaile
'si is cruaidh ni gèum.

The worst cow in the fold
lows the loudest.

The worst people are the noisiest.

Beiridh caora dhubh uan geal.

**A black ewe
may have a white lamb.**

*It is possible to change
for the better.*

Bheir eu-dochas misneachd do'n ghealtair.

Desperation
will give courage
to a coward.

*In dire times
you will become bold.*

Cha d'thug gaol luath
nach d'thug fuath clis.

Quick to love, quick to hate.

*Those who fall in love
quickly fall out quickly.*

Esan nach fuilig
dochainn, cha'n
fhaigh e socair.

He who cannot
suffer pain will not get ease.

*You have to experience
hard times to appreciate
good times.*

Far is sàimhche
an uisge,
ʽs ann is doimhne e.

Still waters run deep.

*A quiet manner
might hide deep passions.*

Far is tainne
an abhain
ʻs ann is mò a fuaim.

Where the river
is shallowest
it will make the most noise.

The loudest person
might not have the most depth.

Is ladurna gach cù air a shitig fhéin.

Every dog is bold
on his own midden.

*It is easy to be overconfident
in your own territory.*

Is i'n dias is truime is
ìsle chromas a ceann.

The heaviest ear of corn
bends its head the lowest.

*The genuinely talented
tend to be modest.*

Theid seòltachd thar spionnadh.

Cunning overcomes strength.

*When you are smart
you do not have to be strong.*

Tha fortan an cuideachd nan treum.

Fortune favours the brave.

*If you are brave
you will create your own luck.*

Labraidh a bheul, ach se'n gniomh a dhearbhas.

The mouth will speak,
but deeds are the proof.

Words are empty,
actions show real intentions.

Bheir aon fhear each
gu uisge ach cha toir
a dhà-dheug air òl.

One man can lead a horse
to the water, but twelve
cannot make it drink.

As hard as you may try,
the stubborn cannot be
persuaded into action.

Bithidh na gabhair
bodhair 's an fhoghar.

The goats will be deaf
at harvest time.

*There's no one as deaf
as those who don't want to hear.*

Cha tig as a phoit ach an toit a bhios innte.

No fumes from the pot,
but from what it contains.

It is what is at the core that is
important, not what is on the outside.

Is bòidhche leis an fhithich a garraiche- gorm féin.

The raven thinks its own chick the prettiest.

You place extra value on what is your own.

Ruisgeadh e a thaigh
fhéin a thuathadh
thaigh a
choimhearsnaich.

He would bare his own house
to thatch his neighbours.

He would do anything for others.

Am fear a gheibh bàs
gach làtha 'se's fhaide
bhios beò.

He who is dying
every day will live the longest.

*Live every day
as if it were your last.*

**Am fear a bhios
beudach e fhéin,
cha sguir e a dh'
èigneachadh chàich.**

He who is guilty himself
will always be urging others.

*The guilty one
always pins the guilt on others.*

Am fear a gheibh
ainm na moch-eiridh,
faodaidh e cadal fada.

He who gets the name
of being an early riser may
take a long sleep.

*Work hard and you'll sleep
better at night.*

Am fear
a sheallas roimhe
cha tuislich e.

He who looks before him
will not stumble.

*If you are aware
of what lies ahead,
you will not be caught off guard.*

Am fear is clis gu
gealladh,
'se's clis gu fealladh.

He who is quickest to promise
is also quickest to deceive.

*Those who do not think before
making a promise
are the first to break it.*

Aithnichear duine air a chuideachd.

A man
is known by his company.

*The friends
we choose define us.*

Am fear is isle bruidhinn 'Se 's fhearr a chluinneas

He who speaks the lowest
hears the best.

It is easiest to pay attention
if you keep quiet.

SELF-IMPROVEMENT
AND
ADVICE

Coin bhadhail
is clann dhaoin eile!

Stray dogs
and other people's children!

*Other people's children
are often an annoyance.*

Abair ach beagan
is abair gu math e.

Say but little and say it well.

*Say only what you need to say
and choose your words wisely.*

Is fhearr a bhi
sàmhach na droch
dhàn a ghabhail.

Better be silent
than sing a bad song.

*It is better to keep quiet
than to talk rubbish.*

Cha toir an uaisle goil air a phoit.

**Gentility
will not boil the pot.**

*Being passive
will not get you far.*

Feuch gu bheil do
theallach fhéin
sguaibte ma's tog thu
luath do
choimhearsnaich.

See that your own hearth is
swept, before you lift your
neighbour's ashes.

*Deal with your own flaws before
pointing out the flaws of others.*

Dean tàir air do
sheana bhrògan
nuair a gheibh thu
do bhiògan ùire.

Despise your old shoes
when you get your new ones.

Do not live in the past.

Mar comas dhuit
teumadh, na ruisg do
dh' eudadh.

If you cannot bite,
do not show your teeth.

Do not argue if you've no point.

Is fhearr a bhi na d'aonar na'n droch chuideachd.

Better be alone
than in bad company.

*It is better to be alone
than to be surrounded by people
with bad character.*

Na sir, 's na seachan
an an cath.

Neither seek
nor shun the fight.

Do not provoke,
but always stand up for yourself.

An luigh nach fhaighear cha'n ì a chobhras.

The herb that cannot be found will not give relief.

If it is not working for you, maybe it is not meant to be.

Am fear is fliuche, rachadh e do'n tobair.

He who is wettest,
let him go to the well.

*The one who is the most accustomed
is the one who is the most effective.*

Am fear nach gheidh
na h-airm 'nam na
sìth, cha bhi iad aige
'n am a chogaidh.

Who keeps not his arms
in times of peace, will have no
arms in times of war.

If you are not prepared,
you will most likely fail.

Am fear a bhios fad aig an aiseig gheibh e thairis uareigin.

He that waits long
at the ferry
will get across sometime.

Be patient.

An ni 's an teid dàil theid dearmaid.

What is delayed
will be forgotten.

*Do not put off things
or they will never happen.*

An rud is fhiach a ghabhail, 's fhiach e irraidh.

If it is worth taking,
it is worth asking for.

If something is worth it,
pursue it.

Bior a d' dhòrn na fàisg;
easbhuidheachd ri d'
nàmhaid na ruisg; ri
gearradh-sgian a d' fheol
na èisd; beisd nimheil ri
d' bheò na duisg.

A thorn in your grasp, do not squeeze;
thy wants to thine enemy do not bare;
the dagger's point to your flesh do not
hear; a venomous reptile do not rouse.

Do not mess with things that will hurt you.

Beus na tuath,
far am bithear
se nithear.

The manners
of the folk
where thou art
thou must adopt.

*Adopt the ways of the people
around you.*

Na spion fiasaig fir nach aithne dhuit.

Do not pluck
the beard of a stranger.

*Do not antagonise
people you do not know.*

Is fhear èiridh moch na suidh anmoch.

Better to rise up early
than to sit up late.

*It is better to start something off early
than to be too late and rush.*

Measar an t-amadan glic ma chumas e a theanga.

The fool may pass for wise
if he holds his tongue.

*If you keep silent
people will not know
you are unwise.*

Is fhearr a bhi marbh
na bhi na d' thràill
reamhar.

Better be dead
than be a fat slave.

*Being free is more important
than being comfortable.*

Buinidh
urran do'n aois.

Honour belongs to old age.

The elderly deserve respect.

CONSOLATION

An rud nach gabh
leasachadh,
's fheudar cur suas
leis.

What cannot be helped
must be put up with.

*What you cannot help
you have to accept.*

Cha d' dhùin dorus nach d'fhosgail dorus.

No door closes
without opening
another door.

There is always hope.

Ged is grinn an sioda is coma leis co air am bi e.

Though the silk be fine,
it cares not who wears it.

*Your appearance
does not define your character.*

Gheibh an t-uaibreach leigeadh an uair is àirde e.

The proud will get a fall when at their highest.

Do not think of yourself too highly or else you will fail.

Cha do shèid gaoth
riamh nach robh a
seòl cuideigin.

No wind ever blew
that did not fill someone's sails.

Every event is good for someone.

Is tric a bheothaich srad bheag teinne mòr.

A small spark
has often kindled a great fire.

*A small action
can trigger a considerable outcome.*

Lionar bearn mòr
le clachan beaga.

Great gaps
may be filled with
small stones.

*Small steps
will lead you to your goal.*

A'chungaidh leighis is goirte, 'si is moth' tha deaneamh feum.

The medicine that hurts the most is generally the best healer.

The most difficult solution is usually the most effective change to 'medicine'.

Cha'n i a mhuc is
sàimhche
is lugh a dh'itheas
de'n drabh.

It is not the quietest sow
that eats the least.

*Meek is not the worst
thing to be.*

Luath Press Limited

committed to publishing well written books worth reading

LUATH PRESS takes its name from Robert Burns, whose little collie Luath (*Gael.*, swift or nimble) tripped up Jean Armour at a wedding and gave him the chance to speak to the woman who was to be his wife and the abiding love of his life. Burns called one of 'The Twa Dogs' Luath after Cuchullin's hunting dog in Ossian's *Fingal*. Luath Press was established in 1981 in the heart of Burns country, and now resides a few steps up the road from Burns' first lodgings on Edinburgh's Royal Mile.

Luath offers you distinctive writing with a hint of unexpected pleasures.

Most bookshops in the UK, the US, Canada, Australia, New Zealand and parts of Europe either carry our books in stock or can order them for you. To order direct from us, please send a £sterling cheque, postal order, international money order or your credit card details (number, address of cardholder and expiry date) to us at the address below. Please add post and packing as follows: UK – £1.00 per delivery address; overseas surface mail – £2.50 per delivery address; overseas airmail – £3.50 for the first book to each delivery address, plus £1.00 for each additional book by airmail to the same address. If your order is a gift, we will happily enclose your card or message at no extra charge.

ILLUSTRATION: IAN KELLAS

Luath Press Limited
543/2 Castlehill
The Royal Mile
Edinburgh EH1 2ND
Scotland

Telephone: 0131 225 4326 (24 hours)
email: sales@luath.co.uk
Website: www.luath.co.uk